THE LITTLE BOOK OF FRIENDSHIP QUOTES

Famous Quotes about Friendship

Compiled by Steve Barnett

Preface

The LITTLE BOOK OF FRIENDSHIP QUOTES resulted from the compiler's need for organization of quotes to use in writing other works. In response to other authors request for access to an easily accessible format to compile quotes, the compiler is publishing this series of quote books rather than producing a large database. All the published quotes can be found in the public domain or fall under the guidelines of "fair use." The compiler's originality exists in the selection, curation, and editing of the work.

I never considered a difference of opinion in politics, in religion, in philosophy, as cause for withdrawing from a friend.

-Thomas Jefferson

It is more shameful to distrust our friends than to be deceived by them.

-Confucius

A man's growth is seen in the successive choirs of his friends.

-Ralph Waldo Emerson

Never contract friendship with a man that is not better than thyself.
                        -Confucius

But friendship is precious, not only in the shade, but in the sunshine of life, and thanks to a benevolent arrangement the greater part of life is sunshine.
                        - Thomas Jefferson

Walking with a friend in the dark is better than walking alone in the light.
                        -Helen Keller

Friendship is the source of the greatest pleasures, and without friends even the most agreeable pursuits become tedious.
					-Thomas Aquinas

Friendship is unnecessary, like philosophy, like art... It has no survival value; rather it is one of those things that give value to survival.
					- C. S. Lewis

Friendship marks a life even more deeply than love. Love risks degenerating into obsession, friendship is never anything but sharing.
					-Elie Wiesel

In everyone's life, at some time, our inner fire goes out. It is then burst into flame by an encounter with another human being. We should all be thankful for those people who rekindle the inner spirit.

-Albert Schweitzer

When we honestly ask ourselves which person in our lives means the most to us, we often find that it is those who, instead of giving advice, solutions, or cures, have chosen rather to share our pain and touch our wounds with a warm and tender hand.

-Henri Nouwen

The friend who can be silent with us in a moment of despair or confusion, who can stay with us in an hour of grief and bereavement, who can tolerate not knowing... not healing, not curing... that is a friend who cares.

-Henri Nouwen

The friend in my adversity I shall always cherish most. I can better trust those who helped to relieve the gloom of my dark hours than those who are so ready to enjoy with me the sunshine of my prosperity.

-Ulysses S. Grant

Remember that the most valuable antiques are dear old friends.

                    -H. Jackson Brown, Jr.

There is a magnet in your heart that will attract true friends. That magnet is unselfishness, thinking of others first; when you learn to live for others, they will live for you.

                    -Paramahansa Yogananda

The sincere friends of this world are as ship lights in the stormiest of nights.

                    -Giotto di Bondone

Friends... they cherish one another's hopes. They are kind to one another's dreams.

-Henry David Thoreau

An excellent man; he has no enemies; and none of his friends like him.

-Oscar Wilde

A friend may well be reckoned the masterpiece of nature.

-Ralph Waldo Emerson

True friendship can afford true knowledge. It does not depend on darkness and ignorance.

-Henry David Thoreau

Rejoicing in our joy, not suffering over our suffering, makes someone a friend.

-Friedrich Nietzsche

It is one of the blessings of old friends that you can afford to be stupid with them.

-Ralph Waldo Emerson

Wishing to be friends is quick work, but friendship is a slow ripening fruit.
                    -Aristotle

In the sweetness of friendship let there be laughter, and sharing of pleasures. For in the dew of little things the heart finds its morning and is refreshed.
                    -Khalil Gibran

Be slow to fall into friendship; but when thou art in, continue firm and constant.
                    -Socrates

Friendship... is not something you learn in school. But if you haven't learned the meaning of friendship, you really haven't learned anything.

-Muhammad Ali

Lots of people want to ride with you in the limo, but what you want is someone who will take the bus with you when the limo breaks down.

-Oprah Winfrey

I want my friend to miss me as long as I miss him.

-Saint Augustine

Be courteous to all, but intimate with few, and let those few be well tried before you give them your confidence.

-George Washington

Friendship improves happiness and abates misery, by the doubling of our joy and the dividing of our grief.

-Marcus Tullius Cicero

An insincere and evil friend is more to be feared than a wild beast; a wild beast may wound your body, but an evil friend will wound your mind.

-Unknown

There are no strangers here; Only friends you haven't yet met.

-William Butler Yeats

One of the most beautiful qualities of true friendship is to understand and to be understood.

-Lucius Annaeus Seneca

I cannot even imagine where I would be today were it not for that handful of friends who have given me a heart full of joy. Let's face it, friends make life a lot more fun.

-Charles R. Swindoll

The bird a nest, the spider a web, man friendship.

-William Blake

A friendship founded on business is better than a business founded on friendship.

-John D. Rockefeller

There is no friend like an old friend who has shared our morning days, no greeting like his welcome, no homage like his praise.

-Oliver Wendell Holmes, Sr.

A friend is someone who gives you total freedom to be yourself.

-Jim Morrison

It seems to me that trying to live without friends is like milking a bear to get cream for your morning coffee. It is a whole lot of trouble, and then not worth much after you get it.

- Zora Neale Hurston

All you need to do to be my friend is like me.

-Taylor Swift

Never explain - your friends do not need it and your enemies will not believe you anyway.

-Elbert Hubbard

One's friends are that part of the human race with which one can be human.

-George Santayana

A true friend is the greatest of all blessings, and that which we take the least care of all to acquire.

-Francois de La Rochefoucauld

You win the victory when you yield to friends.

-Sophocles

Let us be grateful to people who make us happy, they are the charming gardeners who make our souls blossom.

- Marcel Proust

When you choose your friends, don't be short-changed by choosing personality over character.

-W. Somerset Maugham

The world is round so that friendship may encircle it.

-Pierre Teilhard de Chardin

It is not so much our friends' help that helps us, as the confidence of their help.

- Epicurus

I don't need a friend who changes when I change and who nods when I nod; my shadow does that much better.

-Plutarch

One loyal friend is worth ten thousand relatives.

-        Euripides

Where would you be without friends? The people to pick you up when you need lifting? We come from homes far from perfect, so you end up almost parent and sibling to your friends - your own chosen family. There's nothing like a really loyal, dependable, good friend. Nothing.

-Jennifer Aniston

As iron sharpens iron, so a friend sharpens a friend.

-King Solomon

The best time to make friends is before you need them.

-Ethel Barrymore

Each friend represents a world in us, a world not born until they arrive, and it is only by this meeting that a new world is born.

-Anais Nin

Sweet is the memory of distant friends! Like the mellow rays of the departing sun, it falls tenderly, yet sadly, on the heart.

-Washington Irving

True friendship multiplies the good in life and divides its evils. Strive to have friends, for life without friends is like life on a desert island... to find one real friend in a lifetime is good fortune; to keep him is a blessing.

-Baltasar Gracian

Nothing so fortifies a friendship as a belief on the part of one friend that he is superior to the other.

- Honore de Balzac

Our most intimate friend is not he to whom we show the worst, but the best of our nature.

-Nathaniel Hawthorne

A true friend freely, advises justly, assists readily, adventures boldly, takes all patiently, defends courageously, and continues a friend unchangeably.
-William Penn

Friendship needs no words - it is solitude delivered from the anguish of loneliness.
-Dag Hammarskjold

A true friend never gets in your way unless you happen to be going down.
-Arnold H. Glasow

Things are never quite as scary when you've got a best friend.
                    -Bill Watterson

When a friend is in trouble, don't annoy him by asking if there is anything you can do. Think up something appropriate and do it.
                    -E. W. Howe

You find out who your real friends are when you're involved in a scandal.
                    -Elizabeth Taylor

Friends are the siblings God never gave us.

-Mencius

My definition of a friend is somebody who adores you even though they know the things you're most ashamed of.

-Jodie Foster

If instead of a gem, or even a flower, we should cast the gift of a loving thought into the heart of a friend, that would be giving as the angels give.

-George MacDonald

When friendship disappears then there is a space left open to that awful loneliness of the outside world which is like the cold space between the planets. It is an air in which men perish utterly.

-Hilaire Belloc

It is important to our friends to believe that we are unreservedly frank with them, and important to friendship that we are not.

-Mignon McLaughlin

False friendship, like the ivy, decays and ruins the walls it embraces; but true friendship gives new life and animation to the object it supports.

-Richard Burton

If it's very painful for you to criticize your friends - you're safe in doing it. But if you take the slightest pleasure in it, that's the time to hold your tongue.

-Alice Miller

Since there is nothing so well worth having as friends, never lose a chance to make them.

-Francesco Guicciardini

We call that person who has lost his father, an orphan; and a widower that man who has lost his wife. But that man who has known the immense unhappiness of losing a friend, by what name do we call him? Here every language is silent and holds its peace in impotence.

-Joseph Roux

It is only the great hearted who can be true friends. The mean and cowardly, Can never know what true friendship means.

-Charles Kingsley

Silences make the real conversations between friends. Not the saying but the never needing to say is what counts.

-Margaret Lee Runbeck

A friend should be one in whose understanding and virtue we can equally confide, and whose opinion we can value at once for its justness and its sincerity.

-Robert Hall

True friendship is a plant of slow growth, and must undergo and withstand the shocks of adversity, before it is entitled to the appellation.

-George Washington

Sincere friendship towards God, in all who believe him to be properly an intelligent, willing being, does most apparently, directly, and strongly incline to prayer; and it no less disposes the heart strongly to desire to have our infinitely glorious.

-Jonathan Edwards

Friendship with ones self is all important, because without it one cannot be friends with anyone else in the world.

- Eleanor Roosevelt

Friendship, like the immortality of the soul, is too good to be believed.

-Ralph Waldo Emerson

Friendship is two-sided. It isn't a friend just because someone's doing something nice for you. That's a nice person. There's friendship when you do for each other. It's like marriage - it's two-sided.

-John Wooden

Acquaintances we meet, enjoy, and can easily leave behind; but friendship grows deep roots.

-H. Jackson Brown, Jr.

The fact is, with every friendship you make, and every bond of trust you establish, you are shaping the image of America projected to the rest of the world. That is so important. So when you study abroad, you're actually helping to make America stronger.

-Michelle Obama

The rule of friendship means there should be mutual sympathy between them, each supplying what the other lacks and trying to benefit the other, always using friendly and sincere words.

-Marcus Tullius Cicero

I keep my friends as misers do their treasure, because, of all the things granted us by wisdom, none is greater or better than friendship.

-Pietro Aretino

If a man does not make new acquaintances as he advances through life, he will soon find himself left alone. A man, sir, should keep his friendship in a constant repair.

-Samuel Johnson

We must reach out our hand in friendship and dignity both to those who would befriend us and those who would be our enemy.

-Arthur Ashe

We're born alone, we live alone, we die alone. Only through our love and friendship can we create the illusion for the moment that we're not alone.

-Orson Welles

If we would build on a sure foundation in friendship, we must love friends for their sake rather than for our own.

-Charlotte Bronte

It is one of the severest tests of friendship to tell your friend his faults. So to love a man that you cannot bear to see a stain upon him, and to speak painful truth through loving words, that is friendship.

-Henry Ward Beecher

The strong bond of friendship is not always a balanced equation; friendship is not always about giving and taking in equal shares. Instead, friendship is grounded in a feeling that you know exactly who will be there for you when you need something, no matter what or when.

-Simon Sinek

Of all the things which wisdom provides to make us entirely happy, much the greatest is the possession of friendship.
-Epicurus

Love is flower like; Friendship is like a sheltering tree.

-Samuel Taylor Coleridge

To be capable of steady friendship or lasting love, are the two greatest proofs, not only of goodness of heart, but of strength of mind.

-William Hazlitt

I have learned that friendship isn't about who you've known the longest, it's about who came and never left your side.
-Yolanda Hadid

Friendship is also about liking a person for their failings, their weakness. It's also about mutual help, not about exploitation.
-Paul Theroux

Tis the privilege of friendship to talk nonsense, and have her nonsense respected.
-Charles Lamb

Friendships are the family we make - not the one we inherit. I've always been someone to whom friendship, elective affinities, is as important as family.
-Salman Rushdie

Friendship is a very taxing and arduous form of leisure activity.
-Mortimer Adler

A tree is known by its fruit; a man by his deeds. A good deed is never lost; he who sows courtesy reaps friendship, and he who plants kindness gathers love.
-Saint Basil

I have lost my seven best friends, which is to say God has had mercy on me seven times without realizing it. He lent a friendship, took it from me, sent me another.

-Jean Cocteau

Everybody understands friendship, and friendship is different than love - it's a different kind of love. Friendship has more freedom, more latitude. You don't expect your friend to be as you think your friend should be; you expect your friend just to love you as a friend.

-Carole King